Unlocking the secrets of success

Mastering the 5 Habits of High Achievers

BY

SETH N. TAYLOR

INTRODUCTION 4

PHASE 1 6

Success: a personal Journey 6

PHASE 2 15

HOW HABITS CONTRIBUTE TO SUCCESS 15

PHASE 3 30

How Embracing Failure and Learning from It Can Make You Successful.........................30

Understanding the Benefits of Failure...31

CONCLUSION..36

INTRODUCTION

The path to success is paved with habits. Successful people don't achieve their goals overnight; rather, they cultivate a set of positive habits that enable them to consistently move towards their objectives. Whether it's in business, sports, or personal life, success is not an accident; it's the result of intentional and consistent actions.

In this book, we will explore the habits of successful people and uncover the secrets to their achievements. We will delve into the routines, mindsets, and strategies that enable successful individuals to consistently perform at the top of their game. By examining the habits of some of the most successful people in the world, we will provide you with practical insights and actionable steps to help you improve your own habits and achieve your goals.

Through a combination of research, interviews, and personal anecdotes, we will explore the key habits that underpin success, including goal-setting, time management, self-discipline, resilience, and continuous learning. We will also look at how successful people approach failure, setbacks, and challenges, and how they use these experiences to fuel their growth and development.

This book is not just about theory; it's about putting these habits into practice. We will provide you with real-world examples and exercises to help you develop the habits that will enable you to achieve your goals and live a more fulfilling life. Whether you are looking to advance your career, improve your health, or enhance your relationships, the habits of successful people can help you get there.

In today's fast-paced and ever-changing world, it's more important than ever to cultivate habits that will enable you to thrive. By adopting the habits of successful people, you can position yourself for success, no matter what challenges come your way. So, whether you're an aspiring entrepreneur, an athlete, or simply someone who wants to improve your life, this book is for you. Get ready to develop the habits of success and achieve your dreams!

PHASE 1

Success: a personal Journey

Success can be defined as the accomplishment of a desired goal or outcome. It is the result of dedicated effort, hard work, perseverance, and often, a bit of luck. Success is often associated with achieving a particular level of wealth, status, or recognition, but it can also be personal and subjective, depending on an individual's goals and aspirations.

To understand the concept of success, it is important to consider the different perspectives that people have on what success means to them. For some, success may be defined by the amount of money they make or the level of recognition they receive in their profession. For others, success may be more personal, such as achieving a particular fitness goal, learning a new skill, or improving their relationships with loved ones.

One key aspect of success is that it often involves overcoming obstacles and setbacks. The road to success is rarely smooth or easy, and setbacks are a natural part of the process. Successful individuals often possess a growth mindset, which means they view setbacks as opportunities for learning and growth rather than as insurmountable roadblocks.

Another important factor in success is the role of perseverance and hard work. Achieving success often requires sustained effort and dedication over a long period of time, and successful individuals are often those who have developed the discipline and resilience to stay committed to their goals even in the face of challenges.

Ultimately, success is a highly subjective and personal concept, and what it means to each individual will vary. However, common themes among successful individuals include:

1.   A strong work ethic:

Strong work ethics refer to a set of principles and values that guide an individual's behavior towards their work. It is a combination of personal integrity, commitment, responsibility, and professionalism that an individual demonstrates in their work.

Some of the characteristics of strong work ethics include:

Reliability: A person with strong work ethics is reliable and dependable. They consistently show up to work on time and complete tasks on schedule.

Diligence: A strong work ethic involves a diligent and persistent approach to work. Individuals with strong work ethics are willing to put in the extra effort to ensure that they complete tasks to the best of their ability.

Accountability: A person with strong work ethics takes responsibility for their actions and decisions. They don't make excuses or blame others for their mistakes.

Honesty and Integrity: Strong work ethics are founded on honesty and integrity. Individuals with strong work ethics are honest in their dealings with others and maintain high ethical standards.

Self-discipline: A strong work ethic requires self-discipline. Individuals with strong work ethics have the ability to focus on their work and avoid distractions.

Respect: Individuals with strong work ethics show respect to their colleagues, clients, and customers. They treat others with dignity and consideration.

Continuous learning: A strong work ethic involves a commitment to continuous learning and self-improvement. Individuals with strong work ethics are willing to learn new skills and take on new challenges.

In summary, strong work ethics involve a combination of personal integrity, commitment, responsibility, and professionalism that guide an individual's behavior towards their work. It is a set of principles and values that individuals uphold in their work, and it is essential for success in any career or profession.

2.   A willingness to take risks:

The willingness to take risks refers to a person's propensity to undertake uncertain or potentially hazardous activities or behaviors, even when the outcome is uncertain or potentially negative. It can manifest in a variety of ways, such as starting a new business, investing money, traveling to new places, or trying new things.

While risk-taking can be beneficial and lead to great rewards, it can also be dangerous and result in significant losses. Therefore, an individual's willingness to take risks is influenced by several factors, including their personality, past experiences, social and cultural influences, and the potential rewards and consequences of the activity.

Some people are naturally inclined to take risks and seek out novel and challenging experiences. These individuals tend to be more open to new ideas, willing to explore new opportunities, and comfortable with uncertainty and ambiguity. They may view risks as opportunities for growth and learning, rather than as threats.

Others may be more risk-averse and cautious, preferring to stick with familiar routines and avoid situations with uncertain outcomes. They may perceive risks as potential threats to their safety, security, or financial stability, and prioritize avoiding losses over seeking gains.

Overall, a willingness to take risks can be a valuable trait for achieving success in various aspects of life, such as entrepreneurship, innovation, and personal growth. However, it's important to balance risk-taking with caution and thoughtful consideration of potential outcomes, and to avoid taking unnecessary risks that could have severe consequence

3. A commitment to continuous learning and growth:

Commitment to continuous learning and growth is a mindset that values ongoing personal and professional development. It involves actively seeking out new knowledge, skills, and experiences to enhance one's abilities, broaden perspectives, and achieve personal and career goals.

One of the key components of this commitment is a willingness to learn from mistakes and failures. Rather than becoming discouraged or giving up when faced with obstacles, individuals committed to continuous learning and growth use setbacks as opportunities to learn and improve.

Another important aspect of this mindset is a willingness to step outside of one's comfort zone. This can involve taking on new challenges, pursuing unfamiliar topics or areas of study, or seeking out feedback from others in order to identify areas for improvement.

Those committed to continuous learning and growth also prioritize self-reflection and self-awareness. By regularly assessing their own strengths and weaknesses, they are better able to identify areas for improvement and take concrete steps towards personal and professional growth.

Overall, commitment to continuous learning and growth is a valuable trait for individuals in any field or industry. By continually developing their skills and knowledge, individuals can improve their performance, expand their opportunities, and ultimately achieve their goals.

4. A sense of purpose and passion for what they do:

A sense of purpose refers to the belief that one's life has meaning and that one's actions are directed towards achieving a specific goal or objective. It provides a framework for decision-making, prioritization, and motivation. A strong sense of purpose can help individuals overcome obstacles, stay focused on their goals, and maintain a positive outlook on life.

Passion, on the other hand, refers to a strong feeling of enthusiasm or excitement for a particular activity, interest, or pursuit. It is a powerful force that can drive individuals to excel in their chosen field, overcome challenges, and persist in the face of adversity. Passion can bring meaning and fulfillment to one's life, providing a source of joy and satisfaction.

When purpose and passion are combined, individuals can experience a deep sense of fulfillment and satisfaction in their lives. They have a clear sense of direction, and they are motivated to pursue their goals with energy and enthusiasm. Their passion fuels their purpose, and their purpose gives their passion meaning and direction.

However, it is important to note that not everyone has a clear sense of purpose or a strong passion for a particular activity. Some people may struggle to find meaning in their lives, while others may have a variety of interests but lack a singular passion. It is important to remember that everyone's journey is unique, and it is okay to take the time to explore different paths and discover what resonates with you personally.

PHASE 2

HOW HABITS CONTRIBUTE TO SUCCESS

Habits are the building blocks of success. They are the small but powerful actions we take every day that lead us towards our goals. Whether it's waking up early, exercising regularly, or reading every day, our habits shape our lives and ultimately determine our success.

One of the main ways that habits contribute to success is by creating consistency. When we develop a habit, we are committing to a regular routine and behavior that becomes second nature to us. This consistency helps us to stay on track and maintain momentum towards our goals.

Habits also help to develop discipline and focus. By committing to a particular habit, we are training our minds and bodies to stay focused on the task at hand. Over time, this focus and discipline spill over into other areas of our lives, helping us to stay focused and productive throughout the day.

In addition, habits can also help to build self-confidence and self-esteem. When we set a goal and achieve it through consistent habit-building, we feel a sense of accomplishment and pride in ourselves. This positive reinforcement can help to boost our self-esteem and give us the confidence we need to tackle bigger and more challenging goals.

Finally, habits are essential for long-term success. By building healthy and productive habits, we are setting ourselves up for success in the long run. Habits help to create a strong foundation for our lives, giving us the tools we need to achieve our goals and live a fulfilling and successful life.

Success is often attributed to innate talent or luck, but in reality, success is largely the result of habits and behaviors that can be developed over time. By adopting the habits of successful people, you can improve your chances of achieving your goals and living a more fulfilling life. Here are five habits of successful people that you can start implementing today:

1.   Set Goals and Prioritize Them

Setting goals is an important first step, but it's just as important to prioritize them and create a plan to achieve them. Start by identifying your long-term and short-term goals, and then break them down into smaller, more manageable steps. Prioritize these steps based on their importance and urgency, and make a plan to tackle them in order.

To make your goals more concrete and achievable, try using the SMART goal-setting framework. This stands for Specific, Measurable, Achievable, Relevant, and Time-bound. By creating goals that are specific, measurable, and time-bound, you'll be more likely to achieve them.

HOW TO SET GOALS

Setting goals is an important step towards achieving success in any area of your life. Here are some steps to help you set goals:

Identify what you want to achieve: The first step in setting goals is to identify what you want to achieve. This could be anything from improving your health to starting a new business.

Make your goals specific: Once you have identified what you want to achieve, make your goals specific. For example, instead of saying you want to improve your health, you could set a goal to lose 10 pounds in the next three months.

Make your goals measurable: Your goals should be measurable so that you can track your progress. For example, if your goal is to lose 10 pounds, you can measure your progress by tracking your weight each week.

Set a deadline: Setting a deadline for your goals will help you stay motivated and focused. For example, if your goal is to lose 10 pounds, you could set a deadline of three months.

Write down your goals: Writing down your goals will help you commit to them and make them feel more tangible. You can also refer back to your written goals when you need motivation.

Break down your goals into smaller steps: Breaking down your goals into smaller steps will make them feel more achievable. For example, if your goal is to start a new business, you could break it down into steps like conducting market research, creating a business plan, and registering your business.

Create a plan: Once you have broken down your goals into smaller steps, create a plan to achieve them. This could involve creating a schedule or to-do list, finding resources or support, and tracking your progress.

Remember, setting goals is just the first step. It is important to take action towards your goals and make adjustments along the way as necessary.

HOW TO PRIORITIZE YOUR GOALS

Prioritizing your goals is an essential step towards achieving success and fulfillment in life. Here are some steps to help you prioritize your goals effectively:

Identify your goals: Make a list of all the goals you want to achieve. This could include personal, professional, or financial goals.

Categorize your goals: Group your goals into categories such as short-term and long-term goals, personal and professional goals, or financial and health goals.

Evaluate the importance of each goal: Consider the impact each goal will have on your life and how achieving it will bring you closer to your ideal life. Consider which goals are most important to you right now and which ones can wait.

Assess the urgency of each goal: Determine which goals have a specific deadline or require immediate attention. Prioritize these goals over others that may not have a deadline.

Consider the resources required: Determine which goals require more resources, such as time, money, or support. Prioritize goals that you have the resources to accomplish.

Review and revise regularly: Review your goals regularly and adjust your priorities as needed. Your priorities may change over time as your life circumstances change.

Remember, prioritizing your goals is a personal process and requires self-awareness and introspection. By taking the time to assess your goals and prioritize them effectively, you will be better equipped to achieve success and fulfillment in life.

2.   Cultivate a Growth Mindset

A growth mindset is the belief that one's abilities and intelligence can be developed and improved through hard work, dedication, and perseverance. This idea, developed by psychologist Carol Dweck, suggests that individuals who adopt a growth mindset are more likely to achieve their goals and overcome obstacles because they see failure as an opportunity to learn and grow, rather than a reflection of their innate abilities.

In contrast, a fixed mindset is the belief that one's abilities and intelligence are fixed traits that cannot be changed or developed. This can lead individuals to avoid challenges and give up easily in the face of obstacles because they believe their abilities are predetermined and cannot be improved.

Research has shown that individuals with a growth mindset are more resilient, persistent, and motivated than those with a fixed mindset, and they are more likely to achieve success in both academic and personal pursuits.

Adopting a growth mindset means viewing challenges and failures as opportunities for growth and learning. To cultivate a growth mindset, start by reframing your negative self-talk and replacing it with positive, growth-oriented language. Instead of saying "I can't do this," try saying "I haven't figured it out yet, but I'm working on it."

Another way to cultivate a growth mindset is to seek out feedback and criticism. Rather than fearing criticism or rejection, embrace it as an opportunity to learn and improve. Listen to feedback with an open mind and be willing to make changes as needed.

3.   Practice Self-Care

Practicing self-care means taking care of your physical, mental, and emotional health. This can include things like:

Regular exercise

Regular exercise is an important aspect of maintaining a healthy lifestyle. Engaging in physical activity on a regular basis can provide numerous benefits for your physical and mental health.

Here are some of the benefits of regular exercise:

- **Improved cardiovascular health:** Regular exercise can improve the health of your heart and blood vessels, reducing the risk of heart disease, stroke, and high blood pressure.

- **Increased strength and endurance:** Exercise can help you build and maintain muscle mass and improve your overall fitness and endurance.

- **Weight management:** Regular exercise can help you maintain a healthy weight and reduce the risk of obesity.

- **Improved mental health:** Exercise has been shown to reduce symptoms of depression and anxiety and improve overall mood.

- **Reduced risk of chronic diseases:** Regular exercise has been associated with a reduced risk of chronic diseases such as type 2 diabetes, certain cancers, and osteoporosis.

To reap the benefits of exercise, it is recommended that adults engage in at least 150 minutes of moderate-intensity aerobic activity or 75 minutes of vigorous-intensity aerobic activity per week. Additionally, strength training exercises should be performed at least two days per week.

It is important to consult with a healthcare provider before starting a new exercise routine, especially if you have any underlying health conditions.

Healthy eating

Healthy eating refers to consuming a balanced diet that provides your body with the nutrients it needs to function properly. This includes eating a variety of foods from all food groups in appropriate portions, and limiting the intake of foods that are high in saturated and trans fats, added sugars, and sodium.

A healthy diet should consist of:

- **Fruits and vegetables:** These are rich in vitamins, minerals, and fiber, which are essential for maintaining good health.

- **Whole grains:** These include foods like whole-grain bread, pasta, and brown rice. They are rich in fiber, vitamins, and minerals.

- **Lean proteins:** This includes foods like poultry, fish, beans, and tofu. These foods are good sources of protein, which is important for building and repairing tissues in the body.

- **Healthy fats:** These include foods like nuts, seeds, avocado, and olive oil. They are rich in unsaturated fats, which can help lower cholesterol levels and reduce the risk of heart disease.

It is also important to drink plenty of water and limit the intake of processed foods, sugary drinks, and alcohol. Additionally, practicing mindful eating and listening to your body's hunger and fullness cues can help you maintain a healthy relationship with food.

Getting enough restful sleep

Getting enough restful sleep is crucial for maintaining good physical and mental health. Here are some tips for achieving restful sleep:

- **Stick to a consistent sleep schedule:** Try to go to bed and wake up at the same time every day, even on weekends.

- **Create a relaxing bedtime routine:** Take a warm bath, read a book, or practice relaxation techniques like meditation or deep breathing.

- **Avoid stimulating activities before bedtime:** Avoid using electronics, watching TV, or engaging in activities that can cause stress or excitement.

- **Create a comfortable sleep environment:** Keep your bedroom dark, quiet, and cool. Invest in a comfortable mattress and pillows.

- **Limit caffeine and alcohol intake:** Avoid consuming caffeine and alcohol in the hours leading up to bedtime, as they can interfere with sleep.

- **Exercise regularly:** Regular physical activity can help promote restful sleep, but avoid exercising too close to bedtime.

- **Manage stress:** Find healthy ways to manage stress during the day, so that it doesn't interfere with your ability to sleep at night.

Remember, getting enough restful sleep is important for your overall health and wellbeing. If you are struggling to achieve restful sleep, consider speaking with a healthcare professional for further guidance.

Practicing self care can also mean taking time to do things that bring you joy and relaxation, whether it's spending time with loved ones, pursuing a hobby, or simply taking a bubble bath.

To make self-care a regular part of your routine, try scheduling it into your calendar just like you would any other appointment. Make time for self-care activities every day, even if it's just for a few minutes.

4.   Stay Organized and Focused

Staying organized and focused also means developing good habits around time management, prioritization, and productivity. Use tools such as calendars, to-do lists, and project management software to help you stay organized and focused on your goals. Prioritize your tasks based on their importance and urgency, and set realistic deadlines for completing them.

To avoid distractions and stay focused on your goals, try implementing time-blocking. This means scheduling specific blocks of time for focused work and avoiding distractions during those times. Turn off your phone, close your email, and focus solely on the task at hand.

5.   Embrace Failure and Learn from It

Embracing failure as a learning opportunity means reframing your mindset around failure. Rather than seeing failure as a personal setback or a sign of incompetence, view it as a natural part of the process of growth and learning.

To learn from failure, take the time to reflect on what went wrong and what you can do differently in the future. Use this knowledge to adjust your approach and try again.

How Embracing Failure and Learning from It Can Make You Successful

Failure is often seen as a negative experience that we should avoid at all costs. However, failure can actually be a valuable opportunity for growth and learning. Embracing failure and learning from it can help you become more successful in both your personal and professional life.

Understanding the Benefits of Failure

When we fail, we are forced to confront our mistakes and weaknesses. This can be a difficult and uncomfortable experience, but it also provides us with an opportunity to learn and grow. By analyzing our failures, we can identify areas where we need to improve and develop new strategies for success.

In addition, failure can help us build resilience and perseverance. When we experience setbacks, we are forced to push through adversity and keep moving forward. This can help us develop the mental toughness and determination that are essential for success in any field.

Learning from Failure

To truly benefit from failure, it is important to approach it with a growth mindset. Instead of dwelling on our mistakes or beating ourselves up over our failures, we should focus on learning from them. This means taking a step back and analyzing what went wrong, what we could have done differently, and what we can do better in the future.

One effective way to learn from failure is to seek feedback from others. This can help us gain new perspectives and identify blind spots that we may not have been aware of. By listening to constructive criticism and taking it to heart, we can use our failures as a springboard for growth and improvement.

The Importance of Persistence

Embracing failure also requires persistence. It is easy to give up when things don't go according to plan, but true success requires perseverance in the face of adversity. When we encounter obstacles or setbacks, it is important to stay focused on our goals and keep pushing forward.

One way to cultivate persistence is to set realistic goals and break them down into manageable steps. By focusing on small, achievable milestones, we can build momentum and stay motivated even when things get tough.

In conclusion, failure can be a valuable opportunity for growth and learning. By embracing failure and learning from our mistakes, we can develop resilience, perseverance, and a growth mindset that are essential for success in any field. So the next time you encounter a setback or failure, don't be discouraged – use it as an opportunity to learn and grow.

It's important to note that developing new habits takes time and effort. It can be difficult to break old habits and establish new ones, but with consistency and dedication, it's possible. Start by focusing on one habit at a time and commit to making it a part of your daily routine. Once you've established a new habit, move on to the next one and continue building on your progress.

Remember that success is not just about achieving specific goals, but it's also about the journey and the habits and behaviors that lead you there. By adopting these five habits of successful people, you'll not only improve your chances of achieving your goals, but you'll also improve your overall quality of life.

Success Is A Result Of Habits & Behavioural Patterns.

Success is largely the result of habits and behaviors that can be developed over time.

Studies have shown that successful people tend to have specific habits and behaviors, such as setting goals, practicing self-discipline, taking risks, and developing a growth mindset. By adopting these habits and behaviors, you can increase your chances of achieving your goals and living a more fulfilling life.

One key habit of successful people is setting clear goals and prioritizing them. This means identifying what's most important to you and creating a plan to achieve it. By breaking your goals down into smaller, more manageable steps, you can stay focused and motivated.

Another important habit of successful people is practicing self-discipline. This means doing what needs to be done, even when you don't feel like it. It means making sacrifices in the short term to achieve long-term goals.

Successful people also tend to take risks and embrace failure as an opportunity for growth and learning. They view failure as a natural part of the process, and use it as a chance to adjust their approach and try again.

Finally, successful people tend to have a growth mindset. This means believing that your abilities and intelligence can be developed through hard work and dedication. It means embracing challenges and seeking out new opportunities to learn and grow.

By adopting the habits of successful people, you can improve your chances of achieving your goals

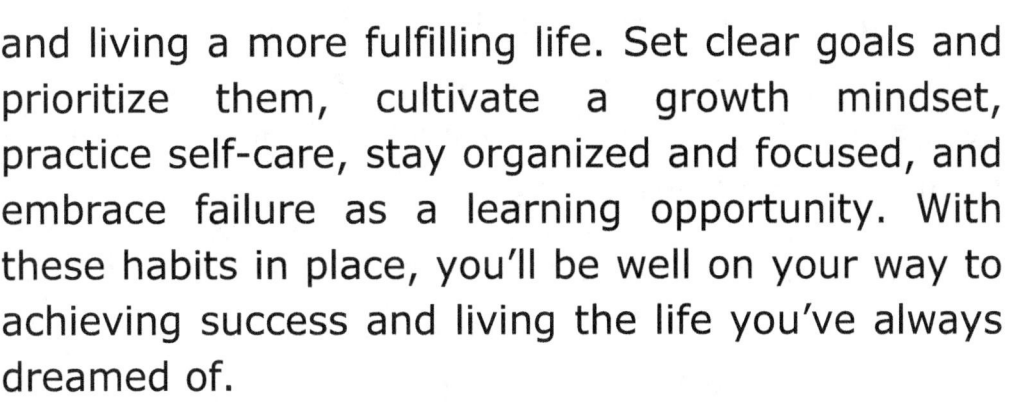

and living a more fulfilling life. Set clear goals and prioritize them, cultivate a growth mindset, practice self-care, stay organized and focused, and embrace failure as a learning opportunity. With these habits in place, you'll be well on your way to achieving success and living the life you've always dreamed of.

CONCLUSION

The book "unlocking the secrets of success" provides a comprehensive understanding of the principles and practices that contribute to success. Through its exploration of the habits and routines of highly successful individuals across various industries, the book offers valuable insights and actionable advice for anyone seeking to achieve their goals and ambitions.

One of the key takeaways from the book is the importance of having a clear vision and purpose. Successful people are often driven by a strong sense of purpose and a clear understanding of what they want to achieve. By setting specific and measurable goals, and then aligning their actions and behaviors with those goals, successful people are able to stay focused and motivated over the long term.

Another critical factor highlighted in the book is the importance of developing positive habits and routines. Successful people understand that their daily actions and behaviors play a critical role in shaping their outcomes, and they prioritize building habits that support their goals. From daily exercise routines to regular reflection and self-assessment, successful people are intentional about their habits and consistently work to cultivate those that will help them achieve their desired outcomes.

The book also emphasizes the importance of resilience and adaptability. Successful people recognize that setbacks and challenges are inevitable, and they are prepared to persevere through difficult times. They understand that failure is not a final outcome, but rather an opportunity to learn and grow, and they approach challenges with a growth mindset that allows them to adapt and overcome obstacles.

Overall, "unlocking the secrets of success" is a valuable resource for anyone looking to improve their personal and professional outcomes. By highlighting the habits and routines of highly successful individuals, the book offers practical advice and actionable strategies for cultivating the mindset and behaviors that lead to success. Whether you are a student, an entrepreneur, or a seasoned professional, this book provides a roadmap for achieving your goals and realizing your full potential.

www.ingramcontent.com/pod-product-compliance
Lightning Source LLC
Chambersburg PA
CBHW071123220526
45467CB00004B/2021